yce Peseroff

HE HARDNESS SCALE

Library of Congress Catalogue card number 77-82224
ISBN 0-914086-18-9

Printed in the United States of America

Cover collage by Ralph Hamilton

I would like to thank the University of Michigan Society of Fellows,
whose support was essential to the completion of this book.

My grateful acknowledgement to the editors of the magazines in
which many of these poems first appeared: *Aspect; Barataria Review;
Green House; Hanging Loose; Iowa Review; The New York Quarterly;
Ploughshares; Salmagundi; Second Wave; Tens; Zeugma.*

Typeset by Ed Hogan/Aspect Composition,
66 Rogers Ave., Somerville, Mass. 02144

The publication of this book was supported by a grant from the
National Endowment for the Arts, Washington, D.C., and assisted
by the Massachusetts Council for the Arts and Humanities.

Alice James Books are published by Alice James Poetry Cooperative, Inc.

Alice James Books
138 Mount Auburn Street
Cambridge, Massachusetts 02138

CONTENTS

1

2

*for my
mother
& father*

1

THE HARDNESS SCALE

Diamonds are forever so I gave you quartz
which is #7 on the hardness scale
and it's hard enough to get to know anybody these days
if only to scratch the surface
and quartz will scratch six other mineral surfaces:
it will scratch glass
it will scratch gold
it will even
scratch your eyes out one morning—you can't be
too careful
Diamonds are industrial so I bought
a ring of topaz
which is #8 on the hardness scale.
I wear it on my right hand, the way it was
supposed to be, right? No tears and fewer regrets
for reasons smooth and clear as glass. Topaz will
                    scratch glass,
it will scratch your quartz,
and all your radio crystals. You'll have to be silent
the rest of your days
not to mention your nights. Not to mention
the night you ran away very drunk very
very drunk and you tried to cross the border
but couldn't make it across the lake.
Stirring up geysers with the oars you drove the red canoe
in circles, tried to pole it but
your left hand didn't know
what the right hand was doing.
You fell asleep
and let everyone know it when you woke up.
In a gin-soaked morning (hair of the dog) you went

hunting for geese,
shot three lake trout in violation of the game laws,
told me to clean them and that
my eyes were bright as sapphires
which is #9 on the hardness scale.
A sapphire will cut a pearl
it will cut stainless steel
it will cut vinyl and mylar and will probably
cut a record this fall
to be released on an obscure label known only to aficionados.
I will buy a copy.
I may buy you a copy
depending on how your tastes have changed.
I will buy copies for my friends
we'll get a new needle,
a diamond needle,
which is #10 on the hardness scale
and will cut anything.
It will cut wood and mortar,
plaster and iron,
it will cut the sapphires in my eyes and I will bleed
blind as 4 A.M. in the subways when even degenerates
are dreaming, blind as the time
you shot up the room with a new hunting rifle
blind drunk
as you were.
You were #11 on the hardness scale
later that night
apologetic as
you worked your way up
slowly from the knees
and you worked your way down
from the open-throated blouse.
Diamonds are forever so I give you softer things.

THE DARK LADY OF THE SONNETS

I am the Dark Lady of the Sonnets, hiding
under the bold striped awnings
of a thousand lovers, their muscled, working arms
waving like flags whose colors
amaze me; I wear my dresses cut low
and my skirts high
in honor of the colors. Everyone knows
my turf, the parked car, and each flag
salutes my dark beret as I ride with the guerrillas,
carry a pistol and grow
my own garden with the help of those who say:
    That lady
    has black lashes
    glittering like rain, like rain
    striking pavement.
and:
    That guerrilla
    can persuade with her dark hair.
    She is, she most truly is,
    wonderful.
Yes I am the Dark Lady of the Sonnets,
slipping back into my secret populations
when the mission is done. I know all the Fords
and Chevys and Ghias on the block:
they won't betray me
to one another. The headlights of men
cruising by my street wink at me:
they will not betray me.
When the black boots come kicking down the door
and ask:
    Who is this woman
    who grows her own garden?

the pavement will collapse beneath them, the earth
will not betray me.
Look—
haven't you been guessing about me for centuries
and centuries to come? But the poets
will never betray me. I am the Dark Lady of the Sonnets,
working hard at the revolution, hard at the wheel,
hard at the turning of a man's head,
the revolution of the heart.

MAKING A NAME FOR MYSELF

It took long enough to get used to
& of course the jokes would piss me
off. Just yesterday a letter from Famous Writer's
Beauty Salon addressed J. Peteroff,
some crazy castrating bitch
the mailman assumes lives here.

When I was young & fat I guessed
each couple pondered & made up the family
name. Such a democrat,
I selected Silvergold, a rich sounding,
solid name. Why didn't my parents
pick Silvergold? So I pondered change & a fat bridal.

My grandfather was tailor to the Czar.
His sons, producing nothing but girls
& homosexuals, leave us alone
with his name. When he got off the boat,
his good wide pants wrapped double & up
to his sunken chest, he cut the "sky",
meaning "Jew", from his name
and walked proud with a solid Russian label
in a land where Russian meant "Jew".

Grandfather, you were out of step
but your name is comfortable as an old shoe
except when I make appointments at Monsieur's salon
or a restaurant sometimes I'll give my husband's,

White; I used to say, W.C. Williams.

HIS MARRIAGE (NOTES FOR A NOVEL)

He is kept circling airport
after airport, while his woman
goes through the atlas, alphabetically.

They were married in the fall.

He loves her and gives her
a ticket
to prove it.

They are beautiful as a football team.

This is not a roman-à-clef.

Lake Michigan never makes a guest
appearance, though each night the Pacific

meets him
like a special agent,
full of secrets and intent to kill.

She turns in her sleep
when this happens,
and never gets pregnant.

WHEN YOU'RE GONE

My hands turn up
in the Lost & Found. All they want to do
is sail into your clothing
like autumn. At night

I curl and cower in my bed like a wolf,
I flail my arms like a pet pigeon,
something in my sleep
is clearly worth escaping.

At the foot of the bed,
a row of mutant vegetables:
nobody's shoes but my own.

LOVE POEM

What is there
to see any more? An arm
is just a hole in the sky,
the mouth,
a cloud.

Candles bite the air as a hand,
not yours,
offers them; I accept
these the way
I accept furniture.

Listening for the rhythms of theft
I think of you but find
the actual burglar
is beating me with sticks.

FUCK POEM

The rooms live on.
When we finish, they continue,
the walls creating the same space,
holding the same air that held
our bodies when we
held our bodies,
preserving the scene
when we have abandoned it
for some novel sunset, some television,
dinner at a friend's.
The bed is forced into it.
The lamps compose themselves in darkness,
the turntable turns at 33 1/3 revolutions
per minute for hours
after we have forgotten the problem,
and I think it's amazing.

ANATOMY

1

If a man likes a woman
with large breasts,
we say he wants his mother.
If he prefers
a woman with small breasts,
we say he wants a boy.
No woman is average there.
She may reach medium height, have normal intelligence,
be middle-aged,
but her breasts
are always melons
or lemons.

2

A man without a penis
may prove a perfect lover,
says Albert Ellis,
but the woman who wants him,
we all agree,
is out of her fucking mind.

TEQUILA SUNRISE

You wear me out
bending me as if there wasn't enough to go around
you, or you had just one night to fill your questionnaire.
What kind of party is this anyway?

Outside the Milky Way
is wrapped like a collar on a deep blue throat,
and the pines lie flat and invisible against the Sierra.
Tomorrow it can't rain.

Your sisters are beautiful too.
And so is your father, and the house he built,
and the roads leading up to the house,
black slate and red slate and veins of granite slab,

I can see them all
projected forward, from the brain, as I hold
your head in my hands.

But we don't stay that way for long, and if others
        can hear us
above the music, in our creaky bed,

nothing's stopping anyone.

THIS POEM IS FOR YOU

1

In an exotic desert city you have forgotten
by now, there is fruit
spread on a white cloth, open
and washed in sand.
The cloth is a cloud
pinned to the table. The lamp is lit:
it is night
and the city is vanishing into a cloud
of touching
& eating grapes. The fruit
is for you.

2

An old man walks home. He measures his step
in constellations. It is too dark
to visit. He sings to his dog. Morning and work
are a long way off and not worth worrying about
when you are walking home
listening to the echoes of your own dry heart
beat mixed
with the patter of a running dog,
or so he thinks.

3

Can you remember the smell of grapes
that slide down your fingers
when you pick them? Or when there is no table,
having dinner in your two hands?

4

The old man spits out his teeth when he speaks
as if to defy a world
that shows he is old. It is the air here that shrivels
        the flesh,
or it is done by eating too many grapes:
Can you still hit
a running dog?

5

I have a map that shows all the ways a dog can go
when fleeing an old master. The map is for you.

6

Clouds hang like drapery at the ends of the world
and I think the world must have
many endings. Here they are very domestic.

Somewhere else there is a bazaar that sells
all you could ever hope to lose. That is
another ending.

7

I have shown you a few rooms.
It's not much
but I call it a home. It is all for you.
The table is for you, and if there is
no table today
that is also for you. The old man, I put in
for you and though the air is free I call
it yours. This poem is for you.

EQUINOX

In the Earsdon sword dance
the father is killed by three healthy sons
but as they strip him of his deerskin robe
he rises with a smile of recognition
and they end up going out on the town and drinking
till 5 A.M.
                On the
Boothbay road
three mechanics with flashlights
leap through a wet and rocky field
back to the pumps
drunk yet elegant,
each one confident
as a man who has sold his life to the movies.

NEW HAMPSHIRE WEEKEND

It is raining.
It is as if the rivers were carefully taken by hand,
and the creeks,
and pressed into nets of mist
we cannot escape. Forms of water
demand attention: we check the tires,
the brakes, the bridges, turn off the highway
in thunderstorms, stay away from trees,
look at each other, try to remember
the best ways of travel
do not depend on weather.

It has stopped raining.
In the tourist cabin Mt. Washington looms
like an unmailed postcard stuck in the window
        behind the bed.
Insects bang listlessly against the screens.
The single bulb sits fat
and dull as a sparrow.
The door slams, the bulb snaps off, you are here
again, again
we touch each other, make preparations, build
bridges in the dark, accept
gifts that are gifts
of water, to be taken carefully by hand
and pressed into nets we cannot escape.

2

.

EXPLORER

The coast is given:
harbors, invented
and kept secret like the yards of your intestine.
On the map
your shoes define year after year
there are places you lingered
until the mad sails touched you and turned you
away. There were islands
inhabited only by vegetables and old friends
who melted unobtrusively into stone the moment
you forgot. Fishermen who loved you
more than their traps, and who told stories
about you like the Virgin of Guadalupe.
Welcomed first as Cortez,
then driven off for having no murders
to write home about, no city waits up for you.
Your compass had a hard night: now
there is only the sun
performing each night the simple dive
that is a suicide's dream.
You think you are the first to notice this.
It is what you are paid for.

FOR MY FRIENDS AWAY FROM AMERICA

Because I have no sense
of history, no holy family
ghosts or grounds or mansions dispossessed,
but my personal cast

of Ten Most Unforgettable Characters,
I want to gather Billy Beano, Johnny-Black-Eyed-
Simpson like greens for the table
from a garden grown over

& the blackberry gone to seed.
I want to call long distance
find out about jobs & work
kids & no kids, what passes

for love in that country
remote as Russia in 1914.
When I think of you
I think of immigrants on the treacherous boat

between desolation & desolation,
one familiar as a playful Cossack
frying the butcher in his own house,
the other the loss

of a talent for smelling smoke.
Your yarns I substitute for family fables,
tales of Chaim Yankel's escape
replaced by the one about submarine

watching in Flushing Meadow Park.
I want to draw you
out of the soil of dirty work,
alien ports, the thick talking

in tongues, the angels away
somewhere in this blue country
of cows & vapid grass stuck
in Jesus' back pocket.

FLORIDA

Every morning the knife dipped
into skin resilient as human
skin & sliced an orange into six
star of david parts. My grandmother
believed in vitamin C
& entered a promised land friendly
to lemons, limes, citrons, tangerines,
balmy with sea smells, mild as God
at the breakfast table
in her third floor walkup.

She kept a picture of her mother—
elegant, a little tired around the mouth—
displayed on the Harmony upright
but I never saw Granpa
who went coconuts & lost
his shirt, his snakeskin
shoes, his vest, the deed
sewn into the vest for 100 acres
of prime Miami waterfront
in a draw game with Lucky & Lepke.

She told me never cross a picket line
one day on Allerton Avenue she refused to enter
    Woolworth's
she didn't know why the coloreds were marching
but remembered friends using petticoats
for parachutes as they jumped from the burning factory
like so many fleas.

Always look on the bright side she told me.
Her husband died. She looked over pages of piano
exercises & said at least I have my music.
Her son died. She said in Germany
I would be dead with my son.
Her second husband prospers
& they buy a condominium in Florida.

I see them twice a year—
each time her hair is a little lighter
his skin a little darker. He is a talker
& my grandmother listens, quiet after all
the years of instruction, prohibition, exhortation.
I see slides of Florida returned to their proper

box, the case snapped shut,
the screen dismantled, the projectionist led away,
the audience eager to talk
about television, taxes, anything but this.

A BAD NEIGHBORHOOD

All the men look funny
and they look at me funny.
Even the women squint sideways.
Is it my *kasha varnishkas?*
The parking lots look friendly—
do they still say that, somewhere?
Does anything want to be here?
Or is this talk in a foreign language
an attempt to make matters quaintly European?
That woman is saying,
"You always wanted a vegetable for a father,"
which sounds better in Italian.
I think it is charming that the boys all carry blades
dipped in tetanus. Or is it their sisters?
These streets are confusing: I think that sign says
"Yellow Mold"
or "Claustrophobic Throat Quarantine"
like a plaque in the botanical gardens.
And where are the botanical gardens?

WILHELM REICH IN FOREST HILLS

*The way of the underground train
is perilous,* rocks the caption
above the tired woman,
her hair tucked under a cerise kerchief,
green coat folded over her lap. Two straphangers
lurching & staring at her legs, whispering,
and she's afraid to look back
at anything but the Doublemint Twins,
toothy & cheeky all the way in
to Queensborough Plaza.

Trees line a boulevard
of Parisian importance and nod to the Pope
on his way from the airport. No butcher hawks his
        koshered meat,
no truckload of fruit idles at the curb, the fruit man
in his cap and apron,
and they never did, not now, not forty years before
when Wilhelm Reich walked among them
and cured their cancers.

IN THE PARK

The benches are in formation.
They will escape to Canada.
It's raining. Up north, it's snowing.
Don't forget your umbrellas!

Waking on these benches
is like strolling through a Mexican garden
not recognizing a single tree or gaudy flower:
still, you are happy to be there.

And the inscription, John + Mary 4-ever,
cropping up in national forests too.
How many Johns over how many sweating Marys?
        And you say
there are no conspiracies.

The benches line up
along the paths of hitchhikers
waiting for the big lift. They pull in their shadows
like patient fishermen each morning,
like invitations rescinded
and replaced with orders to move on.

WEATHER

I don't like watching the news.
Today's thefts have nothing to do
with yesterday's; there is no
brotherhood of victims,
no handshake of loss.
It is as unexpected
as love, as private,
indifferent as California
to Iowa's harvest queen.

But the weather, earth's continuing serial,
binds us all
with questions asked in every language:
        What is the weather today? It is fine.
        Or, It's sunny. It rains. There is fog.

Yet there is no conflict of national interests:
Italian weather for the Italians.
Canadian weather for the Canadians.
We don't meddle even with Cuban weather.

And if we watch the horizon with the care
we give to reading directions, or music,
we prepare for weather one city down the road
as for an old, expected, if uninvited, guest.

RAIN

Nobody likes the rain.
Newscasters apologize,
bringing up a personal anecdote to show
it's no fault of theirs, this rain,
their picnics were washed out,
golf games cancelled,
be kind.

Children are kept indoors like geraniums.
There is too much they might forget,
and they are so busy forgetting.
Whose toy is this? Whose left shoe?

You can follow its progress on this simple map.
It is a curtain drawing shut. Tomorrow
it will be here and here. The birds know.
They huddle in the trees,
decorations for a year already gone.

And the mariners furl the sails
and wear their colorful slickers.
Grave in their boats they listen to the arguments
they know best, another chapter
in the adventures of water.

THE POOL

July heat unwinds from the pavement
as though from the core of the earth.

Next door, the neighbor's pool is open,
the tarp peeled back like an eyelid.

Even if I don't look
I can hear the slap of bodies hitting the water,
imagine the yielding of the surface
to the diver's hands, and then
the pool's interior blue,
meant to reflect water's true color.

Still I sit indoors, sweating, smoking,
the radio in sync with the rippling heat.
I'm not an outdoor person. I used to be
an outdoor person, a good swimmer. Once in a
        Florida motel
I would jump in, climb out, jump in again, regular
and sure, like practicing for the Olympics. It was
an Olympic pool.

The neighbor's is much smaller. When his children tire
they run inside, leaving innertubes to float,
Cheerios in a big, blue bowl.

THE GEESE

"Not habit forming
in proper doses"—so my experience
tells me, and it is an embarrassment
to miss Southern California.
To love the same sun
that turns the green grass brown,
the haze that makes the continuing episodes
of Sunset over the Pacific
worth following
is an obvious mistake,
an error in perception, like taking the clear bottle
for the color of its contents.

What is left are bare walls
and a new face explaining the news.
An eastern exposure is good for plants
and I hear that cold is necessary for growth
in sycamore, elm, maple.

If the geese fly here
they do not need my attention
and it is wrong for me to give it.

PROTEIN

1.
Tuna fish for breakfast
Tuna fish for lunch
Beer for dinner

does not make a good life. Look—
I haven't made many demands.
Never wanted a mansion in the south.
But after a while the desire for protein seeps out of the
              body
and becomes an ectoplasmic hunger
filled by fire escapes, looney tunes, strange men:

January the 12th: swallowed three goldfish, one hard luck
              story,
a tuna fish sandwich.
Rust that walked thru the window
I could handle in no other way.
The rust contained iron. The story was lovely
but lacked proper nourishment.

January the 13th: Vomited.

2.

I am a mushroom fancier
lost in the San Joaquin hills
where it never rains
and fungus doesn't merit irrigation.
I am lost among important things:
jobs and money, mostly,

neither of which surpass the white caps
of mushrooms hidden under a few, wet leaves.
Leave, I say to myself,
saddle up and ride into the sunset
to the stranger you fancy, or California,
the north this time, where mushrooms

pop like bombs after each rain
and cover the earth with spores
making the days brown,
taking root in the sky, even,
becoming stars.
The Great Bear

(so an Indian legend goes)
is a series of inverted mushrooms,
mushrooms fancied by the spirits
and gathered to heaven forever.

Some mushroom fanciers are better
at these things than others.

3.
Dear tree—
we look so much alike. Each of us
has moss growing on the north side,
neither of us
can move far
in any direction.
When I lean out the window, introducing the air
to my face, showing the sun grandchildren
in my hair,
I note a family resemblance.
Dear tree, let us exchange names and addresses.
I have friends in Michigan and California
who would get along well with you.
Let me arrange first class passage, roots and all,
let me do the impossible with you
as I can with no one else. Tree,
I can tell by looking at you
—the way you drop your leaves in winter,
the way you compliment the street
the way Chester's Bar and Grille does not—
you've been picked up before
and by the same old line.
What better reason
for both of us to be here,
for both of us to shake.

THE NEIGHBORS CELEBRATE SPRING

The neighbors celebrate spring.
A lawnmower ratchets across a lawn,
the cop looks handcuffed to his machine.
Women fly flags of laundry
& dry hair in a prison of pink
rubber rollers.
The smell of burnt flesh pleases
the guest at the barbeque prepared
on a japanese altar.
The whole neighborhood is praying
to the TV weatherman
some want sun for the beach
some want rain for the peas.
High school girls fornicate rain
or shine or play tennis
in dazzling white sneakers.
At night the men sit out after work
with beer, cigars, gin rummy,
droll stories about trouble
so hard it would break a man
less a man. Then come stories
about fights & after fights,
women. Soon the cigars bloom
like carnations in the dark
& petals of smoke float up to heaven
deceptively crowded with stars.

BURNT MEADOW MOUNTAIN

Their names are harsh as breath
in winter, these tin-roofed towns—
South Hiram, Brownfield,
Effingham Falls.
No marble minuteman theatrically
guarding the common, no common,
no corn here, and not yet the promised
ski paradise on Burnt Meadow Mountain.
Their highways sprout in summer,
roots edging the tarmac back to the soil,
back to the woods. On a firetrail
cut fresh last year lilacs
crowd like tourists
in Rome among the deer, jackrabbit and beaver,
while folk wait for men with offers,
dreaming the sweet names
of Deauville, Fountainbleu,
and the hot, flat acres of Florida.

FROM THE TOP OF
BURNT MEADOW MOUNTAIN

From the top of Burnt Meadow Mountain
the cemetery looks bigger than the town
and probably is.
White stones sprouting from the earth
like teeth, the dead will come back
to worry us. All ghosts are hungry.

Once I lived in a haunted house.
Windows rattled,
doors were misplaced. My bedroom spun
around and around, and I woke with all the furniture
above, leaning in, like nervous relatives:
"Why did you set Granpa's wig on fire?
Why do you dig up Uncle's pet dogs?
How could you hide the spiders?"

On top of the mountain the air is blue
and sings with the coming storm.
I don't know the words
but I know their alphabet:
all the sounds
of spits, worts, hacks, blears, chokes, and spews.

Clinging to bare rock
with slim arterial vines
the blueberries swell from purple to black.
Ripe and soft
they pop into my hands, sweet
little blue eyes.

Farmers work the fields
behind the graves. Their longhaired sons
go with them, tying back their hair with vines and day lilies.
Later they split a case of beer
remembering ancestors
who also split a case of beer
after a day's work, before a hot August rain.

LAKE OSWEGO

Lake Oswego, Oregon
is not Lake Oswego, New York

yet the same little ghosts danced above them,
suggesting the naming of names to
different pioneers,
one worrying over the British and the corn,
the other, Vladimir, employed
searching out beaver shit and longing for
his mother, and home.

I wonder if he came upon it dreaming
of white Russian nights:
women gliding in sleighs, like comets
across rivers locked and shining as a palace door
                                ?Did he
slap his horse, race the friends
he saw in fir trees right through
the open window of Oregon waters
and awake,
sudden and drowning,
to shout the only word he'd learned in passage
through New York:
                "Oswego!
                Oswego!"

STORM KING MOUNTAIN

The Hudson,
drowned river,
snaps its tides toward the moon while
an owl regards the effortlessness
of flight and settles
his wings slowly.
Below the furrowed
brow of hills people sleep
together, comfortably,
under patchquilts and blankets from Afghanistan.
Hello down there.
I have plans for you (stoned as I am),
I see great things for us
if we stick together.
The darkness, an animal
caught out of its skin, is drawing
on me, a lute,
a violin, and this minute as I talk to you
the stars grin down at me,
knowing the joke
yet playing along.

I pretend to see nature as it is:
endless
as the paths of snails, indestructible as canyons.
But you in Dutchess County know how fragile
is this Storm King. Storm King.
Consider the name.
Consider the wonder of young Bronx boys
and how they must have rolled down their farm denims
and pissed grandly from the top.
Remember the day you took home movies
of young Jack in his hobnail boots
and Protestant blue eyes.
The perfect energy of stars cannot match his played-back
        smile!
Or, the Association of Yachting Clubs of Greater New
        York
choosing this site for the annual regatta:
the pride you felt in varieties
of mapletrees! Forget the city freaks who camp here
and find in the simple acts of earth
a kindness sudden as the wing of an oriole
caught on a chill, cloudy morning.

The sun
is beginning to spread through the hills, now
I'm cold, sitting here
King of the Empties. The campsite
has a pump that must be primed

and I can feel
the pulse along my arms
as I lift the headdress to my head
and singing, singing,
start to pound the drum.

3

POEM

Sometimes when
the sun is
perfect as
an apple in a still-
life with oranges,
and clouds are all
coming home to
me, like horses, the way
I want them,
and the city is far
enough away
for once, the ocean
no longer
a lost coffin to be
prayed over constantly,
I remember we
will never get out
of this alive.

MUTATION

1.

Just because he was singing
a few poems translated from the Norwegian
was no reason
to shoot him. He was in good condition:
fine bones, teeth, hair
that did not fall out if you
ran a finger through. He was tall
enough for most people.
It is true
he was the first to show
this new mutation
of fine down growing from his dorsal muscles:
but even this was no reason
to eliminate one of our finest translators.

2.

A boy in the swamps
crawling through stumps, his fists
like cattails at the end of a stalk, stalks
a tree toad. At the twitch of a finger
the toad flies into a tree.
The boy looks up, his hair
trailing like Spanish moss.

3.
In the alley they're trying to get
this cat. One kid is piling bricks but
he's not allowed to look at the yellow eyes
smoking in the alley—that is not his job.
Someone else can hold that stare.
Here pussy, he grins, showing broken teeth.
The tom grins back, showing broken teeth.
The expert moves in. The cat
turns and flaps lazily away.

4.
No one
can understand this new mutation.
Old men who secretly confided:
                    If God had meant us to fly
                    He would have given us wings
have given up on God as just another unruly grandchild.

THE CAPTIVE

Blood is not loyal.
It leaves the body
at the slightest excuse,
by the nearest exit. It is a river's
longing for the great sea,
& our bodies the dams.
Taste the salt. Blood is memory
of jellyfish and sponge, of the embryo
in the form of a fish. Feel the tides,
the winter air pulling our blood
to the surface. Walking as we do,
on the earth, we invent and carry
the captive within us
until the razor,
the glass, the fall from great heights
frees him, and he goes.

CRIPPLES FROM BREUGHEL

1. No Legs

On his rolling platform
he looks up: No legs!
He has learned the importance of eye contact
and stares when he is closest
to men's legs; women's would not be
right for him. Nearest our footstep
he pushes his own wheels and listens,
the rhythm not like a child on skates.

2. No Eyes

Not hollow sockets but the flesh
grown over—not lack of sight
but the quality of blindness:
This is nothing like the pirate's patch
or the mists your grandfather knew.

3. No Arms

No Arms begs with a cup
in his teeth: his mouth.
He is the best looking of the lot,
his empty sleeves somehow like wings.
He cannot steal from us, beat us,
goose us, gesture at our backs; he can still
get out of the way fast enough;
we give him the most.
We give it to him.

APPROACHING ABSOLUTE ZERO

Friends
we are approaching absolute zero
which is a physical concept
which is a concept in physics we have not seen
and if we have seen it
there is no need.
Simply, then,
there is need. When we get to the point
which is a physical concept
when we get to the point of absolute zero
we will be content
to be as we are
the continent of our bodies
now rising now sinking
will be still as the oceans on the moon
rigid as a flag
erect as the physical concept.
Friends
when we enter absolute zero
we will fill its boundaries
we will no longer approach it like the moon
veering into the ocean or the ocean in
to the contentment of the earth.

Still we will come absolutely
to the point of it
and we will feel the point of it
physically
as we need to do
being, as we are,
not content
but under the ocean looking up
like lost continents
or the lost flags of the continents
or the concept of it.

HARDER

Harder & harder to make
decisions. "One egg
or two?" The refrigerator whines.
I stare into my coffee cup,
a film of cream curdling,
& think, "Not me, not me."

Can I choose
my own *poisson*, tell the bad egg
from the good?
I push away my plate.
I push away the table.
A clatter of knives & forks,
the vaudeville trick
with the tablecloth.

Here's another one:
standing on your head & drinking an Orange Julius
to prove the body's stronger
than gravity. O heavy,
O mysterioso life

force, etc. Your head,
not mine.

Harder to tell
who's choice, who's prime.

The refrigerator takes its fill
of cold & mutely
shuts itself off.
Water invisibly
turns to ice. Not me. Not me.

MILO

Milo, where in the world
are you now? You won't
tell me; I can't ask.

No messages with
pink calling cards
that say FUCK YOU
beneath the lamé invitation.
Just a postcard from Algeria:

Milo of Arabia
& then one from Greece
showing a couple
backed against a white wind-
mill, Milo the peasant
and his little peasantina.

You stamp & stubbornly beg
my attention. Am I Mama
and Milo my bad
apple, my onion?
Is it pure
tears you ask for, another woman
sitting in reverie at the edge
of her own bed?

GOOD AS YOUR WORD

Promises, how can we know what's safe
to swear by? You think you're sure
the earth is round; well it's not,
it's a tear, green & mottled

as a pear
admired from heaven. & can you be sure
there is no heaven? Can you remember
the number you dialed

hands shaky, throat stuck
when you figured, "This is it"?
& who can tell
the future

in cards, teas, herbals,
& say, "Today no one fell
out of love with you, not
tomorrow either," who knows

about hours gone the distance
to the next star not
the sun, light-years?
Who is good

as his word is faithful
as a proper noun,
a person, place, or thing.
Which one are you?

CUTTING BACK

My coleus wag their purple tongues
like mean children. I take up
the pruning shears & the black rubber glove
& cut where the woody stem goes soft & green.
I shape what has gone wrong, like a surgeon
or interior decorator. Some cuttings I save
for the garage sale; the rest lie with chicken bones
& soup cans, looking like a mistake,
the child locked in the family freezer.

You say you're going on a diet
though I can pass my hand through your ribs
& play the Lost Chord. You'll survive
on green translucencies of lettuce,
slices of cucumber, sampling the song
of a warrior who eats
the heart of his hero & calls it devotion.

I break a lunch date. Examining myself,
I find a lump under my left breast,
a secret bud next to my heart.
I don't tell anyone.
At night, I plead fatigue; mornings I am up
before dawn. In a week, it goes away.

ANOTHER ROUND

"Where are you going?"
"Out." "Out?" "We're out
of beer."
"I don't want any beer."
"I'll get some wine."

I watched your legs. I was sick
in my stomach, from drinking
& from the bed, a lumpy mattress
two feet off the basement floor.
I think I wanted to smash out
the window, and home,
but I already was.

"I'm at Mark & Pat's."
"I don't feel like driving."
"I have to talk to Mark."
"Which means I'll have to talk to Pat."
"Do what you want." "What I want?"

So much time strung out
on telephones. I hated
the color coordinated avocado
box, the shrill alarm,
the summons to go yet another round.

A carousel rising & falling,
you bobbing away & into sight
& though I was moving just as fast
& the scene behind you
looked familiar, I never caught up.

THE CONTINENTAL DRIFT

I've been listening
and I think I get it. In the beginning
we were all close, shared the ground
cover, the oak and the ivy together, and the palm,
apples growing with oranges on one hill, the same.
Elephants would roam America,
ostriches would settle in France.

But we let go.
Whether it was like quickie divorce
or a file of unanswered letters, unanswerable letters,
or the ocean pleading its special case
to each soft, reliable coast,
we moved apart.
Africa kept the elephants. We got
the lessons of the oak.

Still it is obvious
how the shapes fit: how any map teases.
I try to read things into it. I try to figure
the message of the Alleghenies, the mottled
America that comes to the edge of the Midwest
and freezes:
where everything is portioned and nothing looks casual,
where there is nothing to stop it until the Rockies.

THE BLUE HOUSE

The day opens
its invitation
to the blue house and enters
stumbling
with its burden of light.
We too are awkward guests
surprised in our nakedness·
cactus overcome
by its own flowering once
every hundred years.

Glacial stones lie beneath the house.
They will rise like our hunger
and burst through the floorboards, demanding,

> "Make us the foundation
> of your new lives;
> tell us what you've learned these past
> eleven thousand years."

What can we give
that's truly our own, what fair share
of inward-leaning pines, the coarse grasses,
a man pissing casual diagrams in the snow?

The doors are full
of expectation.
They want to be open
with us. They want us to investigate
the mystery of the leaning chimney,
the puzzle of the three-legged tub,
the rocking chair's revenge.
To go out of doors
is a kind of betrayal
but one as easily pardoned
as any other complication of the plot.

You want to take my picture
in a congress of Nash Ramblers
left in your neighbor's field to figure
their own way out:
cement wheels and sprung upholstery,
fenders buckled, bogged with snow.
I wonder what you will put behind my face
besides the mountains, the mackerel-back sky,
blossoms of rust and mold.

I tell you, every English village with its god of fuck,
King Tup or golden bull, scared these ancestors
                              bloodless & silly.

To stony Maine they came, assured of a hard life
only to find
Housewives for Hire
Wild Wet & Willing
Every Mon Bargain Nite $4 Carload,
acres of sighs,
little lots of passion,
real blood, real tears.

Burnt Meadow Mountain,
Dugway Flat, Peru Mountain pronounced Pee-rue,
disappear into their shadows
behind sagging barns and spired churches,
Uncle Billy beaming prayer into the tilted ear of heaven,
behind industry, steamboilers left gaping like widows,
behind the nameless and empty roads
surrounding the blue house.
Old Blue, old color of refuge,
you accept the givers of explanations,
the experts in wrong direction,
the footsore and boneweary,
the bored, the ones
who need to know how
snow once touched them
with tongues of angels.

Tonight the stars bend
close for a good look.
We waltz at the window,
dressed in our hair,
the darkness will cover
us for a while,
cover your hands and
my knees the way
a house will a man,
a man his cage of bones,
his bones, his heart.